I0180502

Questions You Always Wanted To Ask About Easter Answered

✝

Questions You Always Wanted To Ask About Easter Answered

MARK FERNANDO

The Hermit Kingdom Press
Cheltenham ♦ Seoul ♦ Bangalore ♦ Cebu

QUESTIONS YOU ALWAYS WANTED TO ASK ABOUT EASTER ANSWERED

Copyright © 2005 by Mark Fernando

All rights reserved. No part of this book may be reproduced in any form or by any means, electronic or mechanical, including photocopying, recording, or by any information storage and retrieval system, without permission in writing from the publisher.

ISBN 1-59689-013-4

(USA) Library of Congress Control Number: 2005921062

Write-To Address:

The Hermit Kingdom Press
3741 Walnut Street, Suite 407
Philadelphia, PA 19104
United States of America

Info@TheHermitKingdomPress.com

- - - - -

Hermit Kingdom
12 South Bridge, Suite 370
Edinburgh, EH1 1DD
Scotland

http://www.TheHermitKingdomPress.com

Dedicated to Rev. Billy Graham,
For his wonderful Christian work

"Of Man's First Disobedience, and the Fruit
Of that Forbidden Tree, whose mortal taste
Brought Death into the World, and all our woe,
With loss of Eden, till one greater Man
Restore us, and regain the blissful Seat"

John Milton (1608-1674)
Paradise Lost

Contents

*Questions You Always Wanted
To Ask About Easter Answered*

Question 1:

Did Jesus Really Rise from the Dead?

Answer 1:

Yes, He did.

It is a fact that Jesus Christ rose from the dead on that first Easter Sunday. Matthew 28:5 is a testimony to the Resurrection of Jesus Christ:

> The angels said to the women: "Do not be afraid, for I know that you are looking for Jesus, who was crucified. He is not here; he has risen, just as he said. Come and see the place where he lay. Then go quickly and tell his disciples: 'He has risen from the dead and is going ahead of you into Galilee. There you will see him.' Now I have told you."

This is one of the many passages from the New Testament that testifies to the Truth about the Resurrection of Jesus Christ, the God Incarnate.

A word or two will help in thinking about the Truth as expounded in the Bible. When Christians talk about the Truth of the Bible, we often use the term Biblical Truth. It is a term meant to be descriptive in nature. It is Truth, and it is in the Bible. Thus, it is Biblical Truth.

What does the term, Biblical Truth signify? We must recognize that, first and foremost, Biblical Truth is fact. In the case of Resurrection, it is a fact that Jesus rose from death.

How do we know that Biblical Truth is fact? Let us answer this question by thinking about this from another angle. How do we know that anything is a fact? For instance, how do we know that what we read on the newspaper is factual? To a certain extent, we trust that the newspaper articles are factual. We trust that the journalists are accurately reporting what they observe. In a sense, we are putting our faith in the journalists, the newspaper, and the whole process of news reporting.

Accepting Biblical Truth involves faith as well. The Bible is written by divinely inspired writers. In a sense, they are reporters for God and the Bible is the divine newspaper meant for humanity. If we can read newspapers and trust what is written there, then why should we have a problem about trusting the account of the Bible? Anyone who trusts a newspaper but cannot trust the Bible is somewhat irrational – certainly from the perspective of cognitive process.

Someone may object and say that the newspaper does not report incredible accounts like the supernatural, but the Bible does. They may assert that it is the supernatural, like the Resurrection, that they cannot accept.

On the surface, what they say may make sense. But when we think about it deeper, we can be confident and say that they are in error.

Over a hundred years ago, people would have thought that it was supernatural for someone to fly to the moon. It seemed like a fantastic idea that could not be achieved. But as we all know, the "super-natural" happened. Humans have found a way to travel to the moon because there was always a possibility there. There were natural laws and scientific principles that operated together to make the journey to the moon a reality.

But before the discovery of the natural laws (which were already in place) and the advancement in scientific understanding, what was "natural" and possible seemed impossible and supernatural.

The Resurrection can be seen as being in the same category. The Resurrection seems impossible because we do not have adequate understanding. But just because there are gaps in our knowledge, it does not mean that the Resurrection did not happen. Just because we have never seen anybody rise from the dead personally does not mean that it can't happen or that it didn't happen. In other words, the Resurrection can certainly be a fact, and we should not let our gaps in knowledge of what-is-really-possible get in the way of acknowledging the Resurrection.

The Biblical writers did a faithful job of reporting the Resurrection of Jesus Christ. They are witnesses.

For everyone, therefore, the Biblical Truth of the Resurrection should be seen as factual.

But for Christians, there is more than fact to help us understand the Truth that Jesus rose from death. We can call this, Experiential Understanding.

When a person accepts Jesus Christ as his personal Lord God and Savior, he experiences an inner change. The inner transition involves a cognitive process of decision to accept Jesus Christ as his personal redeemer. The inner conversion also involves the change of heart. Before, he did not love Jesus Christ, but now, he loves Jesus Christ. The cognitive and the emotive work together in his experience of being a Born-Again Christian.

This creates an Experiential Understanding on a personal level. The Born-Again Christian experiences the love of Jesus Christ and that love continues to grow.

Loving Jesus Christ involves recognizing what Jesus Christ has done for him to save him from eternal death. Of course, what we are talking about is the death of Jesus Christ on the cross and the Resurrection.

For a Born-Again Christian, the fact of the Resurrection of Jesus Christ becomes a part of his experience as a Born-Again Christian. He, therefore, goes through a deeper and deeper understanding of the Resurrection.

The Experiential Understanding is a personal process, kind of like falling in love. It is an experience that all true Christians share. There are similar traits to the Experiential Understanding as there are similar traits to someone falling in love. But there is some diversity as well, as is the case in all personal experiences.

One thing is clear, however. Experiential Understanding will confirm in the heart of every true Christian of the reality of the Resurrection of Jesus Christ.

Resurrection has been a great source of encouragement for many Christians throughout history. And until the Second Coming of Jesus Christ, the Resurrection will continue to bring meaningful experiences to Born-Again Christians in the future.

Yes, Jesus rose from death. This is a fact that is very significant for all true Christians and is at the heart of Christianity.

Question 2:

Who Killed Jesus?

Answer 2:

Jews did.

It is Biblical Truth that Jews killed Jesus Christ. The Bible is clear on this point. One passage in the Bible will illustrate the early Christian witness that Jews killed Jesus Christ. It is in the speech of St. Stephen against Jews found in Acts 7:51-53:

> "You stiff-necked people, with uncircumcised hearts and ears! You are just like your fathers: You always resist the Holy Spirit! Was there ever a prophet your fathers did not persecute? They even killed those who predicted the coming of the Righteous One. And now you have betrayed and murdered him – you who have received the law that was put into effect through

angels but have not obeyed
it."

The speech of Stephen is very important because it is a testimony to
what actually happened.

Stephen was speaking at a
time when the memory of the
crucifixion was fresh in the minds of
early Christians. There were many
who actually knew Jesus Christ,
personally, like Luke, who recorded
the account in the Book of Acts.
Stephen was certainly in the generation when there were many eye-
witnesses of the trial of Jesus Christ
and His death on the cross.

It is important to note that
Stephen does not accuse the Romans
of killing Jesus Christ. This is significant on three counts.

Firstly, it is important for
questions of fact. Jews are responsible for killing Jesus Christ and not
the Romans. The guilt lies with Jews.
This fact is important to establish. It
is like if your father was killed by
someone. Would you not want to
know who killed him? If someone
hired a hitman to kill your father, the
one who hired the hitman to kill your

father is responsible and guilty for the murder. In this regard, the fact that Jews killed Jesus Christ is Biblical Truth and ultimate reality.

Secondly, recognizing the fact that Jews killed Jesus Christ is respecting the Bible. The Bible is emphatic in emphasizing the guilt of Jews in the murder of Jesus Christ. To deny the emphatic accounts in the New Testament is tantamount to disrespecting the Bible. Christians have an obligation to respect the Bible, and recognizing that Jews killed Jesus Christ is a fundamental part of respecting the Word of God.

Thirdly, there is the issue of justice involved. Justice demands that the true culprits be named. To blame the Romans for the wrongs committed by the Jews would be unfair and unjust. For the sake of establishing a sense of justice as a principle, it is important to name correctly those who are behind the wrongful action of killing Jesus Christ. The Gospels gives detailed account of the passing of the death verdict against Jesus Christ by the highest Jewish court and the mani-pulation of the judicial process by

Jews to procure death for Jesus Christ. The whole point of the detailed account is to establish beyond the shadow of doubt the guilt of Jews in killing Jesus Christ.

Thus, it is important to recognize that the Bible was integrally interested in passing on the witness that Jews killed Jesus Christ.

What is also important to note in this regard is that it is not only the Christian witnesses who recognize this fact. In Acts 7, we see that no Jews object to the claim. They knew that Jews had Jesus Christ killed. This was common knowledge among Jews as well as Christians. In fact, there are testimonies by Jews in the Jewish religious text of Talmud that affirm that Jews killed Jesus Christ. There is, in fact, a bit of proud note in that account.

Throughout 2,000 years of history, both Jews and Christians have affirmed this fact. The denial of the fact that Jews killed Christ has only really been in the last 50 years and often initiated by Jews themselves. There is, of course, vested interest in why today's Jews may want to rewrite history to their advantage. It is important for us to guard changing the facts of history as recorded in the Bible and in ancient Christian and Jewish texts.

Also, the stoning of St. Stephen to death is an affirmation of the Jewish guilt in killing Jesus Christ. St. Stephen was preaching the same message as Jesus Christ had taught. Jesus Christ had taught that Jews rejected Him, although God had given them the law and prophecy concerning Him. St. Stephen was accusing the Jews of the same thing. The response was the same. Just as Jews had Jesus Christ killed, Jews had St. Stephen killed.

In fact, persecution of early Christians by powerful Jews as well as Jewish masses was not uncommon. The Pharisees, who are the equivalent of the clergy in the context of Judaism, hired people to go out and hunt Christians down. St. Paul, before he was born-again was one such evil man. Before being saved by the grace of Jesus Christ, Paul was Saul the Pharisee, who's main job was to stalk Christians in order to have Christians arrested and even killed.

Early Christians (both Jews who converted to Christianity and Pagans who converted to Christianity) were hated by Jews and were objects of targeted programs of persecution. The persecution stemmed from the fact and reality of Jews having killed Jesus Christ. This is a part of history and Biblical Truth.

It is important for us Christians to be clear on this historical fact. Not only is recognizing that Jews killed Jesus Christ a way of respecting Jesus Christ, who suffered death on our behalf, it is a way to keep the integrity of Truth and Christianity strong.

Question 3:

What Was the Charge?

Answer 3:

Blasphemy and Threat to National Security.

We see from the Bible that there were two main charges against Jesus Christ; namely, blasphemy and threat to national security.

An account of the charge of blasphemy in the Jewish high court can be seen in Mark 14:61b-65:

> Again the high priest asked him, "Are you the Christ, the Son of the Blessed One?" "I am," said Jesus. "And you will see the Son of Man sitting at the right hand of the Mighty One and coming on the clouds of heaven." The high priest tore his clothes, "Why do we need any more witnesses?" he asked. "You have heard the blasphemy. What do you think?" They

> all condemned him as wor-
> thy of death. Then some
> began to spit at him; they
> blindfolded him, struck him
> with their fists, and said,
> "Prophesy!" And the
> guards took him and beat
> him.

When people read this Bible passage, they are surprised by the violence practiced by the Jewish religious leaders. It is horrible how they could use violence against Jesus Christ as if it were a natural thing to do. While it is important to recognize the problem of courtroom violence in the Jewish high court, it is more important to focus on why Jews wanted Jesus Christ dead.

The charge for which Jews were trying Jesus Christ was blasphemy. The punishment sought for the charge was death. The high priest bought the charge against Jesus Christ in the form of a question. The question, in essence, was asking Jesus Christ if He was claiming to be of the same divine substance of God the Father. When Jesus Christ answered in the affirmative, the charge of blasphemy was confirmed in the minds of Jews. Therefore, Jews levied capital punishment on Jesus Christ.

The fact that Jesus Christ is God is fundamental to the Christian faith. In fact, Jesus Christ taught frequently that He is God. Jesus Christ and God the Father are one.

The Nicene Creed is one of the historic Christian documents that organized the principles of the Bible into a coherent explanation. The Nicene Creed outlines effectively what it means for Jesus Christ to be of the same essence as God the Father. All Christians should carefully read the Nicene Creed because it is important to understand and be able to explain effectively the concept of the deity of Jesus Christ.

Jesus Christ is God. The Gospel of John affirms that Jesus Christ is the Word, who existed before the creation of the world. Jesus Christ as God is eternal and infinite. This divine nature of Jesus Christ is essential to understanding the purpose of Jesus Christ's mission to earth in His Incarnation and to the experience of Christian salvation and growth.

For Judaism, Jesus Christ being God is of the greatest offense. The fundamentals of the Christian faith clashed with the fundamentals of Judaism in the Jewish high court. The outcome is easy to understand. The Jewish high court passed a sentence of death against Jesus Christ.

The charge of blasphemy not only inspired Jews to issue death for Jesus Christ, it encouraged persecution of followers of Jesus Christ, who emphasized the same principles as outlined in the Gospels. Insofar as Jews had access to power, political process, and the judicial system, those who aggressively supported the teaching of Jesus Christ that He is God would be persecuted even by official channels of the government.

Besides the charge of blasphemy, Jesus Christ was slapped with the charge of being a threat to national security.

The charge that Jesus Christ was a threat to national security was brought against Jesus Christ in His absence in the Jewish high court.

The Gospel according to John 11:47-53 describes:

> Then the chief priests and the Pharisees called a meeting of the Sanhedrin. "What are we accomplishing?" they asked. "Here is this man performing many miraculous signs. If we let him go on like this, everyone will believe in him, and then the Romans will come and take away both our place and our nation." Then one of them, named Caiaphas, who was high priest that year, spoke up, "You know nothing at all! You do not realize that it is better for you that one man die for the people than that the whole nation perish." He did not say this on his own, but as high priest that year he prophesied that Jesus would die for the Jewish nation, and not only for the nation also for the scattered children of God, to bring them together and

make them one. So from
that day on they plotted to
take his life.

It seems highly strange to us that the
verdict of death against Jesus Christ
for being a threat to national security
is made when Jesus Christ was
absent. It seems like some criminal
collusion of mafia members rather
than the just process of legal
proceedings worthy of a high court.

But this underhanded policy
should not be surprising in light of
the way the court proceedings turned
out in the case where there was a
charge of blasphemy pending against
Jesus Christ. Jewish court figures
and government officials tried to
produce false witnesses and engaged
in other corrupt practices to pass the
death sentence against Jesus Christ.

The charge of being a threat
to national security, in essence, pre-
ceded the charge of blasphemy. But
in both instances, the verdict of death
was issued against Jesus Christ. In a
sense, a double sentence of death
hung over Jesus Christ after the
Jewish high court issued two charges
against Him.

It would be worthwhile to look at the first charge of being a threat to national security in greater detail. The case helps us to understand the corrupt legal process as it pertained to charging and convicting Jesus Christ.

The Gospel of John shows us that the charge was made without clear details or reliable witnesses. The whole of Jesus Christ being a threat to national security is based on speculation.

Jesus Christ is engaging in miraculous activity. In the minds of Jewish high court administrators, this activity of Jesus Christ will lead to a potential attack of Jews and the Jewish nation by non-Jews and powers that were stronger than they.

In other words, Jesus Christ was a threat because of his potential to raise attack of Jews by powerful non-Jews. It was a speculation not found on fact. It was conjecture based on fear. The Jewish high court charged Jesus Christ of being a threat to the Jewish nation and, therefore, they passed a sentence of death against Jesus Christ.

The process of justice and due process were bypassed and tainted in an effort to have Jesus Christ convicted and killed. We see from the Gospel of John that the Jewish high priest made a religious argument that killing Jesus Christ was meant to be in order to bring safety to the Jewish nation and unite the Jews around the Diaspora.

The Jewish high priest tried to make it seem like it was a religious good for Jesus Christ to be killed. The Jewish high priest even uttered a "prophecy" – an official religious pronouncement to get Jesus Christ killed. There was corruption of religion and religious agencies along with the corruption of the legal process.

We can think about why the Jewish high priest and other Jewish civic and legal leaders colluded to charge Jesus Christ of being a threat to national security and had the sentence of death pronounced against him.

One possibility is out of jealousy. Jesus Christ was performing miraculous deeds and winning people to His teaching about the law and righteousness. The Gospel of John 11:45-47 explicitly states the reality of the increase of Jesus Christ's followers prompting an immediate, emergency meeting by Jewish leaders. Jewish leaders may have been upset that Jesus Christ was beginning to set the tone for discussions about righteousness and following God. Jewish religious leaders wanted to hold onto their pull over the populace. They thought they could maintain their power by bringing a charge of threat to national security against Jesus with the result of a death sentence.

A second possibility is that Jewish leaders found Jesus Christ's teachings offensive. This seems highly possible in light of the charge of blasphemy brought against Jesus Christ soon afterwards. It was offensive to Jewish leaders that Jesus Christ seemed to downgrade Jewish religious laws and attack Jewish religious leaders frequently in His preaching. It was offensive to Jewish leaders that Jesus Christ constantly talked about the Kingdom of God and the legitimacy of its rule. It was offensive to Jewish leaders that

Jesus Christ attacked their way of life as unrighteous and bringing down the ire of God. The charge of being a threat to national security was a cover under which to bring the death penalty swiftly and easily against Jesus. In other words, it was a set-up to get Jesus Christ killed quickly.

A third possibility for why Jewish leaders brought the charge against Jesus Christ of being a national threat is because they feared Jesus Christ. They did not fear Jesus Christ because they believed that Jesus Christ was actually a threat to the nation. They feared Jesus Christ because they were afraid that He would take away their popularity among the people and become more influential in society.

It is like Dr. Martin Luther King, Jr. Dr. King did not have official political power, but he was a very influential person. What he said often outweighed what was said even by the US President. There were more than a few who feared him as a result. Some have wondered if it was the FBI which actually killed Dr. King. The spe-

culation is based on the understanding that some people (especially
those who opposed Dr. King's vision)
in political leadership feared Dr.
King's influence.

It is possible that something
similar was the case with Jesus
Christ. Just like FBI would decide
behind closed doors with some influential political leaders to have Dr.
King killed if they wanted to go that
route, influential Jewish leaders
deliberated and decided behind
closed doors to have Jesus Christ
killed because they feared His
influence. It is important to note,
however, that FBI is a security
agency, while the Sanhedrin was
actually a Jewish high court, similar
to an extent to the combination of the
Congress and the Supreme Court.

The charge against Jesus
Christ as being a threat to national
security stuck and drove an active
process to have Jesus Christ killed.

The two charges against
Jesus Christ, on separate judicial proceedings, of being a threat to national security and for blasphemy
resulted, in both cases, in a death
sentence against Him.

With death sentences already passed by the Jewish high court, Jewish leaders manipulated the Roman magistrate to quickly push their sentence of death penalty through the official channels of capital punishment by means of the most humiliating process possible.

Question 4:

What Religious Practices Were Spurred by Easter?

Answer 4:

The LORD's Day and Early Morning Prayers.

The First Easter is very significant for the Christian faith. Besides the celebration of Easter itself, there are two notable Christian practices spurred by Easter; namely, the LORD's Day and early morning prayers.

The LORD's Day is a term which has been used in Christian history to refer to Sunday, the Christian day of worship. The day is called the LORD's Day in recognition that Jesus Christ is LORD. By LORD, we are pointing to the fact that Jesus Christ is God.

The Old Testament refers to God as LORD, or Yaweh in Hebrew. LORD, or Yahweh, is used as a proper name to refer to God, who created the world and guides history. We Christians believe that Jesus Christ, as God the Son, is of the same substance as God the Father (The Nicene Creed). Thus, Yahweh and God the Son are the same. This is nowhere more clear in the first chapter of the Gospel of John, which unequivocally asserts that the Word is with God and Word is God. God the Son is with God the Father in the sense that they are separate "persons" of the Trinity, but both are Triune God. They are one.

Thus, when Christians refer to Jesus Christ as LORD, we are affirming that Jesus Christ is God. Jesus Christ is the God of the Old Testament. Jesus Christ is the God of the New Testament. Jesus Christ is the God of the Bible.

In this light, it would be wrong to think that Christianity started with the New Testament. It is not that Old Testament is Judaism and the New Testament is Christianity. That would be falling into the heresy of Marcion. Marcion was a heretic in early Christian history who emphasized that Christianity is based only on the New Testament. Marcion argued that the Old Testament belonged to Judaism.

Early Christians fought hard to assert that the Old Testament is the rightful sacred text of Christianity. In fact, early Christians argued that the Jews forfeited their right to the Old Testament when they rejected Jesus Christ as God. Christians throughout thousands of years have argued that rejecting Jesus Christ represents rejecting the Truth of the Old Testament and the point of the Old Testament.

Christians throughout history have argued that the Old Testament prophesied about Jesus Christ. The New Testament represented the fulfilment of the Old Testament. The New Testament and the Old Testament are complementary.

This idea that both the Old Testament and the New Testament point to Jesus Christ is affirmed by Jesus Christ Himself in the Bible. In the Gospels, we clearly see Jesus Christ emphasizing that He came to fulfil the Law and the Prophets. One of the reasons why Jews hated him so much was because He kept reminding them that He is God – both of the Old Testament and of the New Testament.

Perhaps, the most exquisite gift an artist has presented to Jesus Christ, emphasizing this point is Handel's *Messiah*. Handel has used the prophetic messages in the Old Testament to honor Jesus Christ and His identity as the Savior God.

The LORD's Day stands along the similar position of glorifying Jesus Christ by boldly recognizing that He is God and that He has fulfilled the Old Testament.

The LORD's Day, therefore, distinctively emphasizes the core Christian idea of the divinity of Jesus Christ and represents a sharp attack of Judaism's refusal to recognize Jesus Christ as God.

The LORD's Day is celebrated on the first day of the week, Sunday, in honor of Jesus Christ. Obviously, Easter is a very important part of the Christian faith. Honoring the salvation work of Jesus Christ by making the primary day of Christian worship on Sunday in remembrance of the First Easter is only natural. The LORD's Day on Sunday constantly reminds us Christians of the First Easter, filling us with hope of Easter that is integral to our Christian faith. Furthermore, we are encouraged to think back at the First Easter and be reminded to be thankful to Jesus Christ, our God, for the wonderful work of redemption He has wrought on our behalf.

There were other practical reasons why the LORD's Day was established on Sunday. It was to emphasize the complete separation between Judaism and Christianity. By rejecting Jesus Christ, Judaism has rejected the Truth and even the Old Testament. Christianity was the rightful guardian of the Old Testament and the Truth of the Old Testament. Not the Jews.

By celebrating the LORD's Day on Sunday as the Christian Sabbath, Christians affirm that Judaism has got it wrong. It is a practical measure to discourage Christians from having anything to do with Judaism. The practical measure of setting up barriers against Judaism was needed because of continual harmful impact of Judaism on Christians.

In the Book of Galatians, St. Paul attacks the Judaizers. There were recent converts to Christianity who wanted to emphasize that Jews require a privileged place in Christianity. They tried to get Christians to respect Judaism and the practices of Judaism. There was a perpetual threat from Judaism to subvert Christianity, even at the time of the New Testament. Such subversive activities by representatives of Judaism and some ethnic Jews continued. Even a few hundred years from the time of the New Testament, we find sermons telling Jewish converts to Christianity not to go to Jewish synagogues. They are born again in Jesus Christ and they have to cut ties with Judaism, which rejects that Jesus Christ is God.

The LORD's Day was a continual reminder to Christians – both Jewish converts to Christianity as well as Gentile converts to Christianity who were favorably inclined to Judaism – that they must keep their focus on Jesus Christ, the LORD of Resurrection. Especially in areas where there are Jews, having Sunday worship services work practically to separate Christian piety from Jewish piety, most visibly expressed on the Jewish Sabbath. (Jewish Sabbath is actually from Sun-down Friday to Sun-down Saturday, although we say that basically it's Saturday.)

By in large, the observation of the LORD's Day on Sunday is universal among Christians around the world, regardless of culture, language, country, or color.

Easter has spurred other Christian practices as well. Although less universal, Easter has encouraged the practice of early morning prayers. It was early in the morning that the news of the Resurrection was broken.

Christians have understood the women who went out to Jesus Christ's grave as prayerful women who were deep in their Christian piety. Early morning prayer celebrates alert Christian piety like that of the women who heard the first news of Christ's Resurrection. And the early morning prayer honors Jesus Christ's early morning Resurrection.

Many Christians around the world practice early morning personal devotion on an individual level. Some Christians around the world celebrate early morning prayers as a collective practice of Christians. In the modern age, Korean Christians are the ones who have faithfully kept up with this experience. Whether it is in Los Angeles or in Berlin, Germany, you will see Korean Christians gathering together for early morning prayers.

But Korean Christians are not alone in the modern age who recognize the importance of early morning prayers. Many non-Korean churches in the United States and in the UK have early morning prayer breakfasts. There is a prayer meeting along with breaking of breakfast. Many US government, civic, and social leaders engage in early morning prayer and breakfast. This is a part of the Christian tradition that recognizes the importance of morning prayers. And the tradition goes all the way back to the First Easter.

Question 5:

What Happened to Jesus Christ's Body?

Answer 5:

Resurrected Body.

It is important to understand that Jesus Christ's Resurrection was a bodily resurrection. What this means is that at death, all the bodily functions stopped functioning as it would with any humans who die, but at the Resurrection Jesus Christ's body started functioning again.

To understand Resurrection correctly, therefore, it is important for us to understand the concept of the Incarnation. What is Incarnation?

The Incarnation was a historic event in time and space, whereby God took on human flesh. Christians often talk in terms of "God became man."

However, it is important to note that God did not relinquish His divine nature or being when He "became" man. God remained fully divine, but merely came to have human form and flesh. Thus, we

Christians have historically talked about Jesus Christ being fully God and fully human.

Thus, while we may talk in terms of "God becoming man," we need to make it clear that Jesus Christ is both God and man. The Council of Nicea and the Council of Chalcedon from the fourth and fifth centuries are very helpful in understanding the divine nature of Jesus Christ from a theological angle. Of course, the Bible is clear on this point.

Although it is very important to emphasize the divine nature of Jesus Christ, it is important to emphasize the human nature of Jesus Christ. In fact, that is the whole point of the Incarnation. Jesus Christ took on human flesh so that he could die.

Obviously, God cannot die. God is neither male nor female. God is eternal in time and infinite in space. God is spirit.

God had to take on human flesh in order that He could die. Human beings can die and do die.

Why is this so important? It is only through the death of Jesus

Christ that we have our salvation. In the historic Christian faith, we have described this idea as substitutionary atonement, or propitiatory atonement.

The basic idea of Propitiation is that Jesus Christ died in our place so that our sins could be forgiven. It is only through blood sacrifice that sins can be forgiven.

In the Old Testament, blood sacrifices were offered regularly in the Jerusalem Temple. The Old Testament describes the function of sacrifices for the forgiveness of sins. The emphasis was that the blood had to be shed in order for there to be forgiveness. This is the rule that God established, as outlined in the Old Testament.

In other words, without the shedding of blood, there cannot be any forgiveness. As this is the established rule set down by God, God has operated in the world in the context of this rule. For human beings to be forgiven, there has to be sacrifices for the forgiveness of sins. When the sacrifices for the forgiveness of sins were not offered, God punished the sinners, directly.

The Old Testament is filled with passages describing God's punishment for sins. God often killed ancient Israelites for their sins. The Bible does say that had they repented, they would not have been killed. But the Bible also accounts how the non-repenting were killed by God.

The killing of ancient Israelites is often described as disciplining. God loved Israelites, so God killed them. God killed some Israelites, so other Israelites would come to repentance and offer proper sacrifices and worship to God. God killed some Israelites so that not all Israelites would have to be killed. God disciplined Israelites by killing them. The Old Testament describes this as a loving act of God the Father.

In the Old Testament, therefore, sacrifices of animals were seen as a sign of true repentance. Those who were truly sorry for their sins would go through the trouble of sacrificing and shedding the blood of a precious animal as the evidence of their genuine spirit of contrition. It is only through the shedding of the animal blood and through the propitiatory sacrifice that God would avert his heavy-handed discipline of killing Israelites.

Sacrifices were evidence of repentance. But it was more than that. Sacrifices of animals in the Old Testament were a picture of the work of redemption by Jesus Christ on the cross.

In fact, it wasn't the blood of the animals that put forgiveness of ancient Israelites into motion. The sacrifices were a type of picture (or typology) of the propitiatory sacrifice of Jesus Christ. It was really the death of Jesus Christ on the cross and his work in substitutionary sacrifice that brought about the forgiveness of sins in the Old Testament.

Thus, Christians often talk about the believers in the Old Testament as looking forward to the work of Jesus Christ on the cross and the believers after the coming of Jesus Christ as looking back at the saving work of Jesus Christ on the cross.

The propitiatory work of Jesus Christ's work on the cross effectuated forgiveness of sins in past-times, in the present, and in the future for all those who believe in the name of Jesus. In a sense, therefore, Jesus Christ's substitutionary work on the cross had a timeless effect in its power to forgive sins.

The sacrifices of the Old Testament were teaching Old Testament believers of the coming sacrificial work of Jesus Christ. It was the substitutionary sacrifice of Jesus Christ that forgave the sins of ancient Israelites, not the Old Testament sacrifices. Old Testament sacrifices were only a shadow of things to come, pointing to the real thing.

This is why Jesus Christ taught in the Gospels that even Abraham was saved by putting his faith in Him. Obviously, Jesus Christ was not incarnated at Abraham's time. Jesus Christ took on human flesh at 0 AD, when He came to earth to fulfil His propitiatory work on the cross. The point is, of course, that although God the Son had not taken on human flesh at the time of Abraham, Abraham still believed in the reality of God the Son that He would take on human flesh and save him through the propitiatory work on the cross, and that was why Abraham was saved.

This is an important principle to remember. Abraham was saved by faith in Jesus Christ who was to come thousands of years after his death. In the same manner, ancient Israelites were saved by believing in Jesus Christ, who was to come to effectuate forgiveness of sins by His substitutionary sacrifice on the cross.

So, it is plain to see why the Incarnation is so important. The whole system of repentance outlined in the Bible hinges on the saving work of Jesus Christ on the cross. In order for God to die, He had to take on human flesh. God cannot die with only divine nature. But when God has both divine and human natures, He can die.

Without the substitutionary death of Jesus Christ, who is God the Son, there is no forgiveness of sins. That is the way God the Creator designed the world.

Jesus Christ, therefore, had a fully human body (although it was without sin). Thus, Jesus Christ was able to die on the cross and did die on the cross.

At the Resurrection, Jesus Christ arose from death. This means that his human body that stopped functioning came to life again.

In death, Jesus Christ's human heart stopped beating. In death, Jesus Christ stopped breathing. In death, Jesus Christ's human organs all stopped functioning.

In other words, Jesus Christ's human body was clinically and scientifically dead in the every sense of that word, death.

In the Resurrection, Jesus Christ's human body came alive again. It means that all the vital functions of the human body started working again. Jesus Christ's human heart started beating. Jesus Christ's human breathing continued yet again. Jesus Christ's human organs started functioning again.

It is important to emphasize the resuscitation of all human functions in the Resurrection. It is also important to note that Jesus Christ's body after the Resurrection was a resurrected body. What that means is that it was no longer the corruptible human body.

Jesus Christ's resurrected human body could not die again. Jesus Christ's resurrected human body could not collapse again. Jesus Christ now had a resurrected body.

The resurrected human body is the same kind of body that we human beings will have when Jesus Christ raises us from death at His Second Coming.

The Bible teaches us that when Jesus Christ returns in all His glory at the Last Days, He will raise everyone from death in order to judge humanity.

Those who have accepted Jesus Christ as Lord God and Savior will enter eternal life in the Kingdom of Heaven, and those who rejected Jesus Christ will enter eternal death in Hell.

With the resurrected body, that is incorruptible and indestructible, all humans will live forever either in Heaven or in Hell.

Those who live in Heaven will live happily forever in the presence of Jesus Christ. Those who live in Hell will live forever in the presence of Satan, the Prince of

Darkness, forever in pain and torment.

It is because of the resurrected body, human beings will be able to live forever.

Jesus Christ's resurrected human body, therefore, gives us a picture of what is to come in the future with dead human bodies.

At the Resurrection, Jesus Christ rose from death in a bodily resurrection with a resurrected body. This is a very important point to remember as it gives us picture into our eternity.

Question 6:

Why Did God Have To Die To Save Humans?

Answer 6:

Because Only
God Is Sinless.

The question – Why did God have to die? – is a very important question. If it was not required that God should die for the sake of the salvation of humans, then there would not have been a need for the Incarnation where God takes on human flesh in order to die.

Obviously, because there was a God-determined rule that God had to die as a propitiatory (substitutionary) sacrifice that God took on human flesh in the person of Jesus Christ as told in the Gospels found in the New Testament.

The reason why God had to die is because God is sinless and only the One who is sinless can die in a substitutionary atonement.

The explanation is simple, really. All human beings are sinful and, therefore, all human beings are guilty before God for their own sins. All human beings have to die for their own sins. The Bible is clear in emphasizing that the wages of sin is death. The guilty cannot save another guilty person as a substitution. That is why a completely sinless Being had to die in substitution. This is where Jesus Christ comes in. He is God, and he took on human flesh. He is completely sinless, and as a sinless God-man, Jesus Christ died as a substitutionary sacrifice. Let us try to understand this principle of the Bible by examining the elements of the Biblical logic in greater detail.

First, let us think about the concept of sin. Adam and Eve were kicked out of the Garden of Eden – because they sinned. Before they disobeyed God and ate of the Tree of the Knowledge of Good and Evil, they owned eternal life.

Their default position was not to experience pain or death. Had they not broken that one rule outlined in the Book of Genesis in the Old Testament, they would have lived eternally. Before their first disobedience, they knew neither sin nor the consequences of sin.

However, when Adam and Eve disobeyed God and ate of the fruit of the Tree of the Knowledge of Good and Evil, they experienced sin. Furthermore, they experienced the consequences of sin. They realized that they were naked. Before then, they did not know their nakedness.

Many commentators of the Bible have noted that this was the point at which sexual sins entered the world. The moment that disobedience corrupted, it corrupted the sanctity of everything, including sex.

The result of sin was clear. In accordance with the principle found all over the Bible that the wages of sin is death, Adam and Eve were punished to experience death.

Adam and Eve were kicked out of the Garden of Eve and they were to experience death. Being that they were the first generation of humanity, every human being after them would experience death.

The wages of sin is death. That was the punishment. It was at that point that elements that lead to death also entered humanity. Sickness leads to death. Before the disobedience of Adam and Eve, there was no sickness because there was no death. But after the disobedience to God's command because of curiosity and the desire to be like God, Adam and Eve were doomed to experience sickness and pain that are a part of the experience of death.

With Adam and Eve's disobedience by eating of the fruit of the Tree of Knowledge of Good and Evil, sin entered the world. We call this sin, the Original Sin. It was the first sin. It was the sin by which the whole created order became corrupted. The Original Sin brought death to humanity.

The Puritans who were persecuted in England and ran away to America have a saying, "In Adam we sinned all." This short saying outlines the principle of the Original Sin.

When Adam and Eve sinned as the first man and woman, their sin became an integral part of humanity. In other words, every human being who is born into this world is born with sin following Adam and Eve.

Theologians have used the term – "imputation of the Original Sin" – to describe the process by which every person who is born is born with sin. It is understood that at the moment of conception, a person has original sin.

In other words, the moment that a sperm fertilizes an egg and the life of a baby begins, the baby has sin. This is the principle of Original Sin. There is an imputation of the Original Sin.

That is why many places in the Bible emphasize the principle that there is no one righteous, not even one. There is no human being who is sinless because the moment that a sperm and an egg unite to create a fertilized egg, the human life is imputed with the sin of Adam.

In this regard, sin is understood as passing from the father to his children via the mother. Thus, Adam is the originator of the Original Sin and Eve was the conduit of the Original Sin as passed on by Adam in the conception.

It is because of the principle outlining the origination of the Original Sin that the Puritans in

America created the catchphrase, "In Adam we sinned all." Notice that it is not, "In Adam and Eve we sinned all."

Some men out there may feel that it is unfair that the first man is blamed for the Original Sin. They may say, "Was it not Eve who tempted Adam to partake of the fruit of the Tree of the Knowledge of Good and Evil? Should not Eve take the primary responsibility for the Original Sin?"

We have to look to the Bible for the answer. It is understood in the Bible that Adam should have refused Eve's temptation and should not have consumed the fruit of the Tree of the Knowledge of Good and Evil. If Adam had not sinned, the Original Sin would not have entered humanity.

The principle that sin entered the world through Adam is clearly outlined in the teaching of St. Paul. It was through the First Adam, that of Adam in the Garden of Eden, that sin entered the world. But it is through the Last Adam, namely Jesus Christ, humans have the opportunity for salvation.

According to the Bible, Jesus Christ is the Last Adam who permanently reverses the effects of Original Sin causated by the First Adam. It is in Jesus Christ, the Last Adam, the corruption put in motion by the First Adam for humanity is reversed. The creation will ultimately be stored to pre-Fall conditions through Jesus Christ.

The language to describe the restoration is found in terms, such as "the New Jerusalem" and "the New Heavens and the New Earth." Jesus Christ as the Last Adam will restore the world to the pure state for eternity. Those who accept Jesus Christ as Lord God and Savior will be restored to the Heavenly Garden of Eden.

It is important to think a little bit further about the Biblical teaching of the Original Sin. It is through Adam that the Original Sin is conveyed throughout humanity. In other words, the Original Sin enters each successive generation by the father.

Thus, if a man marries a woman and they have two sons and two daughters, the Original Sin is imputed into the two sons and the two daughters by the father. The moment that the mother's egg is fertilized by the father's sperm and life begins, the Original Sin is imputed into the child.

To describe in biological terms, the Original Sin is carried through the male sperm. The female egg is neutral – sinless. The female egg is without the Original Sin. The male sperm carries the Original Sin.

Some people may be tempted to ask how this is the case? As a way of explanation, it would be helpful to look at the concept of "the heart." What does it mean to accept Jesus Christ into our heart?

Although we use the term "heart," when we talk about accepting Jesus Christ into one's heart, it does not refer physically to the beating heart in our chest. We use the term "heart" almost metaphorically. However, it is not really a metaphor since there is a space where the reality of the presence of the Holy Spirit occurs.

Similarly, when one falls in love, one feels love. Where does the person feel love? We say we feel love in our heart. When we say this, we do not mean that our love is going on in the organ identifiable as the heart. It is inside of us but we cannot precisely identify this place. We have come to call this unknown realm, "the heart." This is just as real as the beating of the physical heart.

When we think about the imputation of the Original Sin, we can think in this regard. The male sperm carries the Original Sin. It is just as real and actually present in the sperm. However, just like "the heart," it is impossible to identify.

The Biblical principle is clear, however. When life begins at the point of the fertilization of the egg, the Original Sin is imputed into new human life.

That is why the Bible can state unequivocally that there is no human being that is righteous. All human beings have fallen short and are sinful. How can a baby that is just born be sinful? What has he done the moment he is born? The reason that the Bible could say that even the just born baby is not righteous and is with sin is because all human beings are born with the Original Sin.

Why is this understanding of how Original Sin enters the world important? It is important because it relates to the Christian understanding of the sinlessness of Jesus Christ.

Jesus Christ was born as a human being. Jesus Christ through Incarnation was carried in the womb of Mary, like any human child. However, the important thing to remember is that Jesus Christ's human life was not created by the joining of a human sperm and a human egg.

Mary's egg became the carrier of the humanity of Jesus Christ, but a human male sperm played no role. As we have discussed, the Original Sin is carried through the sperm. The female egg is neutral and sinless. Thus, Jesus Christ was completely sinless in the womb of Mary. No male sperm impregnated the egg of Mary.

Protestants have called this principle, The Virgin Birth of Jesus Christ. Catholics call this principle the Immaculate Conception. Although there are differences in language and some conceptualization, the fundamental principles are the same.

Jesus Christ was born sinless because a human sperm did not impregnate Mary's egg. There was an immaculate conception by the Holy Spirit. It was a miraculous conception. It was a conception meant to bypass the process through which the Original Sin is imputed to every human being born of a human father and a human mother. The Original Sin is carried through the male sperm.

Thus, Mary was a sinless vestibule for God the Son who took on human flesh in the sense that her egg was completely sinless. The male sperm, however, is not sinless; it is the carrier of the Original Sin.

It moves us to see all the troubles that God went through to bring us salvation. Only the Sinless could offer a substitutionary atonement for human beings. All human beings are sinful, so no human being could function as a substitutionary atonement.

Because no human being can act as a propitiatory sacrifice, God decided to come down and save all human beings who desired to be saved and have eternal life.

God, who is sinless, cannot die. The problem was solved in that God took on human flesh, so that He could die.

There is the problem of the Original Sin. Thus, God chose to bypass the process by which the Original Sin enters humans. Mary's egg was not impregnated by Joseph's sperm, which carries the Original Sin.

By bypassing the male sperm, God became Incarnate in the person of Jesus Christ without sin. Thus, Jesus Christ, who is God and completely human being in the biological sense of the term, is without sin.

Jesus Christ, the God-man, who is without sin, can die in substitution for humans. All human beings are sinful and deserve death. However, all those who believe in Jesus Christ as God and Savior have their punishment of eternal death taken away on account of the propitiatory sacrifice of Jesus Christ.

Only God is sinless. All human beings are with sin. From the moment of conception, all human beings have the Original Sin. And we continue to commit sin through-out our lives.

God, who is without sin, chose to die as a substitution for us, so now we have the opportunity to be saved on the force of Jesus Christ's propitiatory work on the cross.

We should be thankful to Jesus Christ, who being God, loved us to take on human flesh in order to die for us. Jesus Christ, being God, is the only One who could die as a substitution for us.

Praise be to the name of Jesus Christ!

Question 7:

What Is Eternal Death?

Answer 7:

Endless (in time) Suffering and Taste of Death.

Eternal Death as expounded in the Bible is endless suffering and perpetual experience of what it feels like to die forever and ever.

When Jesus Christ comes back in Judgement on the Last Day as outlined in the Book of Revelations and revealed in the Old Testament prophecies, particularly found in the books of Isaiah and Jeremiah, He will raise the dead to life.

The dead who are raised to life will receive resurrected bodies meant to last for eternity. In the Judgement, Jesus Christ will look at the Book of Life. All those who accepted Jesus Christ as God and Savior have their name inscribed in the Book of Life. The human beings with their name in the Book of Life will be ushered into Heaven to spend the eternity in Heaven. We call this eternal life.

Those whose names are not inscribed in the Book of Life will be sent to Hell to spend eternity with Satan, the Prince of Darkness.

The eternity in Hell will not be a happy one. In fact, Jesus Christ said that there would be gnashing of teeth and crying. It will be painful beyond your wildest imagination. If you can think about the greatest pain in your life experience – whether physical, mental, or emotional – and compound that pain by 10 times, it would not even begin to describe the intensity of the pain and suffering of Hell.

This pain and suffering will go on forever and ever without end. There is no stopping of the suffering. That is why it's called eternal death. It is like dying every day, every moment, and all the time. This excruciatingly painful state of feeling like dying perpetually will not end.

Both those who will be sent to Heaven and those who will be sent to Hell will have resurrected bodies that are forever.

Jesus Christ took up the requirement for everyone to experience excruciating eternal death. All have sinned. The wages of sin is death. Eternal death.

However, Jesus Christ died in a propitiatory sacrifice so that those who believe in Jesus Christ will have the requirement of eternal death taken away. Those who believe that Jesus Christ is God and Savior will have eternal punishment taken away and will be given eternal life as a reward.

The substitutionary sacrifice of Jesus Christ is wonderful. It gives everyone the chance at eternal life. Those who believe will go to Heaven and live with God forever. Those who refuse to believe in Jesus Christ as God will meet eternal death. It is up to you to accept Jesus Christ or reject Jesus Christ. And you will reap the benefits of your decision or suffer the consequences.

When we say that Jesus Christ died in our place on the cross as a substitution, we are saying that Jesus Christ died the eternal death in our place.

You may ask how Jesus Christ died an eternal death when the death on the cross was finite. Furthermore, wasn't Jesus Christ resurrected from the dead?

Yes! Jesus Christ arose from death. Three days after the death on the cross, Jesus Christ rose from death.

So, how is it possible that Jesus Christ died in our place the eternal death that we need to experience on account of our sins? How was Jesus Christ's seemingly finite death an eternal death?

The answer is found in the nature of Jesus Christ. Jesus Christ is fully God and fully human. There is no compromise of the two natures. For the historic Christian explanation of this principle in a systematic form, it would help to re-read the ruling of the Council of Chalcedon in the fifth century AD.

For the purpose of answering this particular question, the divine nature of Jesus Christ is very important. Jesus Christ is fully God. That means that Jesus Christ has all the attributes of God Himself.

What are the attributes of God? God is eternal and infinite. God is all-knowing (omniscient), all-powerful (omnipotent), and present everywhere (omnipresent).

So, while the human form of Jesus Christ was confined in time and space, the divinity of Jesus Christ is never confined in time and space. As God, Jesus Christ is eternal and infinite.

In a mystical and mysterious way, the two seemingly contradictory qualities of humanity and divinity were present in the person of Jesus Christ.

Thus, any death that Jesus Christ died in the human form takes on the qualities of infinite and eternal death. The two natures of Jesus Christ are inseparable. They are not distinctively separate but present in Jesus Christ in an integral way.

In other words, the death of Jesus Christ was eternal in nature by the virtue of the fact that Jesus Christ is God-man who is eternal in His divinity.

To better understand this, it would be helpful to think about the finite death of human beings. We are by nature finite. No human being in the world has eternal qualities of God. That's what separates God from humans. Jesus Christ is the mediator because He bridged the gap by taking on human flesh while being God.

Because human beings are finite, we die a finite death. Our death is finite and limited in space and time because of our nature as human beings. Thus, in order for human beings to die an eternal death, human beings would have to experience the extent of death perpetually forever. Only eternity of time will make human death eternal.

In other words, the only way human beings can die an eternal death is to experience the force of death in terms of time – eternally.

With God, this is different. First of all, God cannot die. That is why Jesus Christ had to take on human flesh in order to experience death. But when Jesus Christ, who is God, took on human flesh, He remained God with the eternal nature of God. Thus, while being able to die after the Incarnation, the death would not be exactly the same. We cannot ignore the divine nature of Jesus Christ.

When Jesus Christ died on the cross, he died in His human form. But that death confined to the finite human space and time was eternal and infinite in nature due to Jesus Christ's divine nature. In other words, in the ultimate reality of things, Jesus Christ experienced eternal death as he died on the cross because He died as God-man.

This is why Jesus Christ's substitutionary death was just that. Jesus Christ was able to take away our punishment for eternal death because He died our eternal death for us.

If Jesus Christ's death was a finite death, it would not be enough to take away the punishment that we have to suffer – namely, eternal death. But because Jesus Christ's death was eternal in nature, it functioned as a substitutionary sa-crifice for our punishment.

When we accept Jesus Christ as our God and Savior, the liability for eternal death is taken away from us. We have passed over from eternal death into eternal life. As

Christians, we no longer have to die eternally; we can now live eternally in Heaven.

This is why Easter is so important to us. Easter represents the substitutionary sacrifice of Jesus Christ on the cross, whereby He experienced eternal death on our behalf, so that if we believe that Jesus Christ is God and accept Him as our Savior, we have eternal life in Him. We no longer have to experience eternal death in Hell.

There is no human being who is righteous. All human beings are sinners, from the earliest conception period of the fertilized egg to the elderly. We all deserve eternal death. The wages of sin is death. Eternal death.

Our sin against God is against an eternal being. The punishment for our sin is eternal and infinite in nature (by the virtue of the fact that the One against whom we committed the sin is God, who is eternal and infinite). The wages of sin is death. The death is eternal death because we sinned against the eternal God.

Jesus Christ's death on the cross was a work of propitiation. Jesus Christ died in our place without sin and not deserving eternal death.

Jesus Christ's suffering eternal death on our behalf has taken away our liability to punishment. When we accept Jesus Christ as God and our Savior, we no longer have to worry about the liability to suffer eternal death.

Jesus Christ has paid it all; all to Him I owe. This is the personal testimony of all who experience salvation in Jesus Christ.

This is the most valuable gift of Easter. Jesus Christ's propitiatory work on the cross gave all true Christians eternal life!

About the Author

Mark Fernando is an experienced Bible teacher who has a gift for expounding complex Bible ideas in simple and understandable language. Mark has taught at many Bible studies in different contexts – in churches, universities, evangelistic programs, and mission fields. Mark's Christian work is mainly located in the United States and the European Union.

`

www.ingramcontent.com/pod-product-compliance
Lightning Source LLC
LaVergne TN
LVHW011211080426
835508LV00007B/724